LIGHTS
DAY AND NIGHT

THE SCIENCE OF HOW LIGHT WORKS

Written by SUSAN HUGHES

Illustrated by ELLEN ROONEY

Kids Can Press

Summer,
a cloudy night,
no moon or stars.

The sky is so dark, then ...

A firefly!

Blink, blink!

Such a tiny insect, but its light glows brightly in the darkness!

Then, a breeze picks up. The treetops bend and sway, and the sky begins to clear.

Oh, look!

The sky is full of stars. They are millions of miles away, but their light travels all the way from there ... to here.

A star is a spinning **ball** of **gases** — made of matter that isn't **liquid** or **solid**. The center of a star is incredibly hot. This heat creates an enormous amount of **energy**, making the star glow!

Blink, blink!

The firefly and the stars are part of nature.
The light they make is **natural** light.

The Sun — which is
also a star — makes
natural light, too.

And there are other kinds of natural light.

Lightning flashing across the sky.

A forest fire.

A volcano.

The northern lights.

When you snuggle down at night to read a bedtime story, do you need a light?

During the day, sighted people can use light from the sun to see.

But sunlight isn't always available.

And no one can see without some kind of light.

Put on a blindfold and sit under a blanket with a collection of small items. Try to identify each item.

How did you do? What would make it easier?
What would make it *a lot* easier?

When there is no natural light, people find ways to make light.

They burn wood, wax or oil.

They use **electricity** to make **artificial** light.

Artificial light needs a source of energy, like electricity. Many of us use electricity to power our lights, keep us warm — and charge our screens!

We use light to communicate.

A lighthouse beam guides ships at sea.

Traffic lights control the flow of traffic.

The scoreboard at a hockey game keeps track of goals.

A flashing light tells you your friend is at the door.

All life on our planet depends on light from the Sun.

Sunlight warms the air, the seas and the land, making Earth a perfect home for us and other living things.

Sunlight is an important part of the water cycle. Sunlight heats water in oceans, rivers and lakes. The water turns into **vapor** — tiny drops of water in the air.

Green plants need sunlight to grow. And plants make the oxygen that we all need to breathe.

The vapor rises into the sky
to fall again as rain. Round
and round it goes.

Without any sunlight, Earth would
be dark and covered in ice. There
wouldn't be any life here at all.

What is light? It's a kind of energy.

It travels out in all directions, but it moves in straight lines. Light travels through space or air until …

... it hits something!

What happens when light hits a solid object, like a cement wall, a book or a metal door?

These objects are **opaque**. They block light from traveling all the way through them.

Many opaque objects **absorb**, or take in, light.

Your body is opaque!

Can you see your shadow? That's your body absorbing light and blocking its path.

And look what happens when an airplane flies over a field. An airplane is also opaque.

You and your friends can make
shadow puppets with light.

pupil

retina

image

optic nerve

But not all light is absorbed into an opaque object. Some of the light **reflects**, or bounces off. That's how we see things.

The reflected light travels through a hole in your eye, the **pupil**, and onto the **retina**, a thin layer of tissue at the back of your eye. This tissue turns the light energy into signals, and the optic nerve carries those signals to your brain.

Aha! Your brain tells you what you are seeing.

Like a mountain in the distance.
Or a cat …

Hey, where's the cat?

So, we can see objects that give off their own light. We can also see objects that reflect light into our eyes.

Now, shine a light through a piece of tissue paper. Why does it look blurry? Tissue paper is **translucent**. It reflects or absorbs much of the light. Only a little light passes through.

When light travels through a window, a little of it reflects off the glass — but most of it passes right through. The glass is **transparent**, or see-through.

Like glass, water is also transparent. Light can pass through it. But when light hits water, it slows down. Just like how water slows you down when you run in a lake or swimming pool. The water also makes the light **refract**, or bend.

Some animals — like cats, raccoons, opossums and owls — have eyes that work better at night than human eyes. They don't need much light to see.

Owls can see better at night than some people do in bright daylight!

A cat's pupils can
open much wider
than human pupils.

This allows their
eyes to take in lots
of light, helping
them to see better
in the dark.

Lighting up the darkness is a
perfect way to celebrate …

And when we turn the lights out,
it's a perfect time to sleep.

Goodnight, lights!

CLiCK

A SHADOW PUPPET SHOW

Stuff you need:

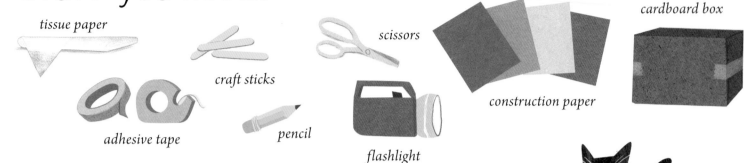

tissue paper

craft sticks

scissors

construction paper

cardboard box

adhesive tape

pencil

flashlight

How to make the screen

1. Cut the bottom out of a cardboard box, leaving a border.
2. Cover the hole with a piece of tissue paper. Tape the paper in place.

an audience

How to make the puppets

1. Draw a simple outline of an animal on the construction paper.
2. Cut out the animal and tape it to a craft stick.
3. Make more puppets, if you want.

It's show time!

Turn the screen to face the audience and shine a light on it from behind. Turn off the lights in the room and start your puppet show!

What happened?

Some light can pass through the translucent tissue paper, so the audience can see through it. Light could not pass through the opaque construction paper, so the puppets make dark shadows on the screen.

WORDS TO KNOW

absorb: to take in or soak up

artificial: made by people and not created by nature

electricity: a kind of energy that is found in nature but can also be artificially produced

energy: the ability to do work. Light is a kind of energy, and the Sun is the main source of energy for Earth.

gas: an invisible substance that isn't a liquid or a solid. Air is made of gases, like oxygen.

light: a kind of energy made of tiny packets of energy that travel like waves

natural: caused by nature and not made by people

opaque: does not let light through. You cannot be seen through it.

pupil: the dark opening in the center of the eye. It widens or narrows to control the amount of light that reaches the retina.

reflect: to bounce back

refract: to bend slightly

retina: a thin layer of tissue at the back of the eye. It turns light rays into signals that our brains understand.

translucent: lets light through but you can't see the objects on the other side clearly

transparent: lets light through so you can see the objects on the other side completely

vapor: tiny droplets of water in the air, like steam. Vapor is a type of gas. It turns to liquid at room temperature.

To my dear friends' grandchild, Jannik Szuchewycz — S.H.
For my dad, who showed me the stars — E.R.

With thanks to physicist James Rabeau of the University of Melbourne
for generously taking the time to review the manuscript.

Text © 2021 Susan Hughes
Illustrations © 2021 Ellen Rooney

Published in Canada and the U.S. by Kids Can Press Ltd.
25 Dockside Drive, Toronto, ON M5A 0B5

Kids Can Press is a Corus Entertainment Inc. company

www.kidscanpress.com

The artwork in this book was made with scissors, construction paper, paints, pencil crayons and a computer.
The text is set in Arno Pro.

Edited by Jennifer Stokes
Designed by Andrew Dupuis

Printed and bound in Dongguan, Guangdong, P.R. China in 03/2021 by Toppan Leefung

CM 21 0 9 8 7 6 5 4 3 2 1

LIBRARY AND ARCHIVES CANADA CATALOGUING IN PUBLICATION

Title: Lights day and night : the science of how light works / written by Susan Hughes ; illustrated by Ellen Rooney.
Names: Hughes, Susan, 1960– author. | Rooney, Ellen, illustrator.
Identifiers: Canadiana 20200369245 | ISBN 9781525303197 (hardcover)
Subjects: LCSH: Light — Juvenile literature.
Classification: LCC QC360 .H84 2021 | DDC j535 — dc23

Kids Can Press gratefully acknowledges that the land on which our office is located is
the traditional territory of many nations, including the Mississaugas of the Credit,
the Anishnabeg, the Chippewa, the Haudenosaunee and the Wendat peoples, and is
now home to many diverse First Nations, Inuit and Métis peoples.

We thank the Government of Ontario, through Ontario Creates;
the Ontario Arts Council; the Canada Council for the Arts;
and the Government of Canada for supporting our publishing activity.

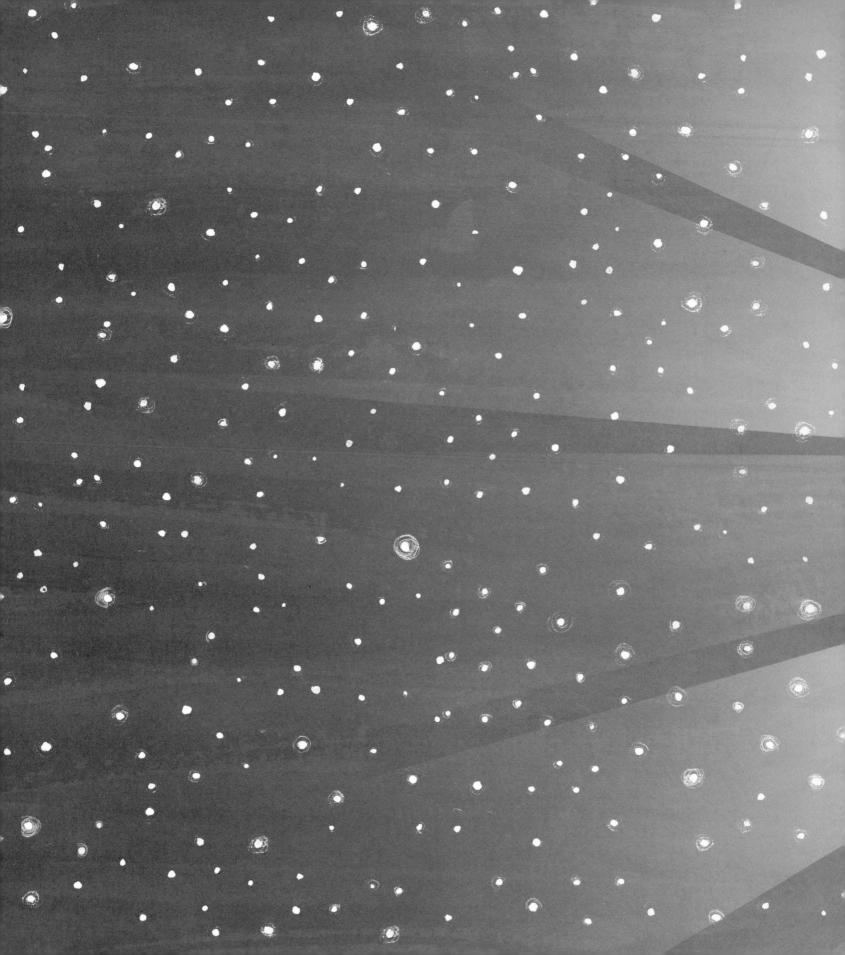